The pigeon who w

At the weekend Daniel decided to teach Victoria to become a "homing" pigeon, and for some reason they decided that she needed to do some high flying first. They took her out onto the roof and threw her out into space. The idea was that she would circle around above them and then return. But instead it was like trying to throw a ball on an elastic string; however they threw her, she would shoot off about eight feet and shoot back just as fast. They gave up—you can't make anything return, they said, that won't go away.

VICTORIA

The biography of a pigeon

by
Alice Renton

IVY BOOKS • NEW YORK

Ivy Books
Published by Ballantine Books
Copyright © 1988 by Alice Renton

First published in 1988 by André Deutsch Ltd.

ISBN 0-8041-0395-X

This edition published by arrangement with André Deutsch Ltd.

Manufactured in the United States of America

First Ballantine Books Edition: December 1988

We seem to have been acquired by a pigeon.

It wasn't exactly intentional but happened, as so many things do, as the result of being in a hurry. Christian and I were running through Victoria Station, dodging among the rush-hour crowds, towards Platform 19, and we both saw it, huddled against the foot of one of the pillars that support the station roof. We stopped, panting, beside it. It had clearly fallen out of a nest somewhere high in the girders above us, and equally clearly it was not going to get back into its nest unaided, even if it escaped being trampled underfoot, which was an imminent danger. It looked like a choice between helping the pigeon and missing the train, or catching the train and feeling guilty about the pigeon. As there was no time to debate these alternatives, Christian grabbed the pigeon, I grabbed her bag, and we all three caught the train with seconds to spare.

Animals have a tendency to happen to us as a family. Tim and I found ourselves to be cat-owners within a month of marriage, and it has gone on like that ever since. Our five children seem to have inherited the failings; Christian, eldest of our three daughters, had during her twenty-one years been responsible for many impulsive additions to our fluctuating menagerie. Lately, with the family growing up and leaving home, the flow has not been so constant. I was aware as we sank into our seats of a sense of déja vu.

Our foundling was not an alluring sight. It was young, small—about the size of a blackbird—and

1

looked dirty. Dishevelled grey-black feathers covered a fair portion of its body, with unattractive naked areas under its wings, as if it had been partially plucked and then discarded as too scraggy for consumption. It hardly had any tail, and there was a lot of pink about its head and beak. Here and there were damp-looking yellow hairs, the remains of down now being replaced by feathers.

It sat on some newspaper on Christian's knee, apparently unafraid, and responding to our hand movement by opening its beak wide and squeaking.

I went to the buffet car and chose an egg and tomato sandwich as offering a varied diet. It was difficult to get the food into its beak, because although it opened avidly as our fingers approached, it shut quickly again before we could get the scraps in. We devised a method of inserting a finger from the side and holding the beak open for long enough. It was messy, but fairly effective.

The little pigeon was really hungry. The bread went down well and was clearly familiar diet, and the tomato was accepted. But the egg was a failure, since the yolk stuck to our fingers and in trying to smear it into its beak we only succeeded in bunging up its nostrils.

Passengers walking past us along the aisle made the little bird squeak excitedly and crane towards the movement. A foreign tourist photographed us from several seats away, and a homeward-bound commuter opposite, after one long, serious look over his glasses, raised his pink newspaper firmly between us.

The discovery of two fleas crawling across the newspaper on which the bird sat, announced in interested tones by Christian, caused a slight diversion on the seats across the aisle, and on the whole it was a relief when we left the train at Lewes.

2

May 2nd

We were quite surprised to find the pigeon fledgling still alive when we came down to the kitchen this morning, not least because Moley, the cat, had spent the night unnoticed asleep in a chair pushed under the dining table. He cannot have failed to notice the scrabbling sounds coming from the cardboard box on top of the table, but for some reason had done nothing about it. Moley was himself a foundling, some fifteen years ago. As a thin black and white kitten he appeared wandering in Moulsecoomb, a suburb of Brighton, from which his name derives.

The pigeon appeared to be starving—it jumped up and down when we appeared, squeaking frantically. Brown bread seemed to be enjoyed even more than white, and we fed it bread pellets, with entrements of tomato, throughout the day, its appetite seeming insatiable. We are getting a little concerned about its diet. Even a British Rail pigeon should surely have some variation on sandwiches. We needed expert advice. With the help of the Yellow Pages we found the name of a pigeon breeder, and rang him.

"You've got a squeaker," he said. "Just give it chicken-mix, and a few dried peas."

So we went to the corn merchants in Lewes, and talked to Vic Blunt, an old friend who has provided advice for us and food for our ponies for years.

"We've got a squeaker," we said, and showed it to him. He gave us two bags, of mixed grain and of dried peas. It seemed an enormous amount for a very small

5

bird that would probably die soon. We tried to pay.

"Don't give me anything," said Vic. "If it lives you'll be back for more anyway."

We did, however, buy some flea powder from him.

May 5th

We are realising that a pigeon of determination like this one is not likely to die. It demands food constantly and has learned, if food is not forthcoming, to climb up the side of the box and knock it over. It prefers, in any case, to walk about the kitchen floor, rushing with wild squeaks at any passing foot. The two dogs, Jess and Cleo, eye it with interest and some suspicion, but so far have not attempted a grab. We try not to expose them to too much temptation, and have found a cardboard box with higher sides. The cat remains entirely aloof.

The likelihood of survival has encouraged the allotting of a name, which obviously had to be Victoria, and which has decided the vexed question of her sex, however mistakenly. Victoria she is.

She had not drunk anything since she came, despite being given frequent opportunities. We rang the pigeon breeder again, and asked if we should worry.

He said, "You hold its head under water for ten seconds and it'll soon drink."

He was right, though my nerve gave after five seconds. Anyway, she now drinks quite normally.

May 7th

There is no question now of keeping Victoria in a cardboard box. She learned very quickly that by flapping her wings and scrabbling with her claws she could upset a box of any height, and thinks there is far more fun on the outside anyway. Christian has introduced her to the garden, which has reminded her that there is more to life than a kitchen.

She is beginning to think about flying, and clearly enjoys jumping from the table to the floor, and seeing if she can land a little further away each time. But she never jumps down if you put her on your shoulder, perhaps because it is still too high for her, but I suspect really because she likes the sensation of riding around at a height.

She cannot yet jump upwards very far, and makes no attempt to fly from the ground. We have taken to keeping her food on the kitchen window seat, out of the way of the dogs. It is only about two feet high, but though she knows her food is there she has to wait for a leg-up.

She is sleeping now at night in a wooden box with a wire grill on a ledge outside the front door. Our second son, Daniel, made it. He and Chelsea, his twin sister, were home at the weekend, and they feel that keeping Victoria in the house too much will soften her up, so that when she decides to leave us she won't be able to cope with the weather. In the morning she squeaks at us through the grill, and then hops onto a shoulder and comes indoors to be fed.

I think Daniel's interest in Victoria is largely prompted by the thought that if she survives to adulthood, and stays with us, she might come in useful. He sees her as an economical, if not entirely practical, link between his lodgings at Durham University and home.

May 9th

Mr. and Mrs. Taylor, two of our nearest neighbours, live in a flint cottage a few hundred yards down the hill. Their son Peter, who visits his elderly parents regularly, heard that we had a pigeon in residence and called on us. He is a good joiner, and was unimpressed by Victoria's box in the front porch. He has made her a proper wooden house, with a pitched roof, which he has fixed to the wall by the front door, about five feet from the ground. She behaved impeccably when he introduced her to it. She was placed on the projecting "doorstep" and walked straight in. She spent about two minutes carefully inspecting the interior before emerging again apparently satisfied with all she had seen. There is a wire door, through which she peers in the early morning, and much more space inside than in her box.

She enjoys following us in the garden, and pays close attention when I am weeding. I put her on the edge of the wheelbarrow, where she sits happily as I push it around, but prefers apparently to sit on my shoulder, occasionally dropping to the ground, but then coming close to be lifted up again. As I bend to the ground to pull up groundsel and bindweed she walks about on my back, clawing her way back to my shoulder as I straighten up. I wonder what she thinks I am.

May 12th

In the last few days Victoria has effectively taught herself to fly, and it has been fascinating to watch her developing ability. Since she had no other bird to copy, and I was not prepared to run in front of her flapping, the process has, I imagine, been slower than it would normally be. There has, for a start, been no motivation: apart from her initial premature fall from her nest in Victoria station she has not fallen, or been pushed, from any height; nor has she needed to look for food, which has always been brought to her, or her to it. Any wanderlust that may encourage young birds to leave home has been satisfied by travelling about on our shoulders, or being carried, or just walking, since neither the dogs nor Moley bother her. Certainly there has been no danger to encourage her to take the air. So she has simply discovered for herself that flying is both possible and fun, and what is more she makes it look fun.

It started two days ago when I took her to the plantation below the house. This area was planted with young ornamental trees about five years ago, and they will soon be ready for sale. Recently I have been labeling and retying them in anticipation of the rush of eager customers I hope for in the autumn. I put her on the wooden fence and started work on a row of trees about thirty yards away. She walked to and fro along the fence for a little while, and then jumped off in my direction, flapping hard. To our mutual surprise she managed to keep airborne for a good eight yards before hitting the grass. She scuttled over to me, hopping over the grass tufts, and you could almost imagine her saying, "Did you see? Did you see what I did?"

I took her back to the fence, where she waited until I had returned to where I had been working, and then tried again. This time she got a little further before touching down, and when she joined me I took her back again. Each time she waited till I had got back to where I had been, the tree work now taking second place to this excitement. Eventually she remained airborne over the whole distance, flapping frantically and dropping lower and lower, skimming the grass over the last few yards, before she landed at my feet. I felt her triumph, like that of a child who has finally swum across the shallow end of a swimming pool without putting a foot down.

By the next afternoon she could take off from the ground for low flights of up to twenty yards, and today she was beginning to fly upwards from the ground, onto the wheelbarrow, and even onto the kitchen table.

After a week in London, Tim returned home as usual on Friday night and was amazed at Victoria's development. I think he thought that by now there would be another small bump in the little animal graveyard under a big beech tree in front of the house, where less successful rescue stories of the past have sometimes ended.

May 13th

Victoria nearly came to an untimely end today. She
was basking in the sun, lying on the cushion of one of
the garden chairs. She lies down a great deal, it seems
to me, for a bird. In any case, my mother-in-law, who
has been staying for the weekend, didn't see her, and
decided to sit down. A frantic shriek from me narrowly
saved Victoria from becoming *pigeon pressé*. In the
event, she kept the chair.

May 16th

She can fly reasonably well, now, but only in relatively straight lines. Not being able to take corners accurately in flight makes her life in a house full of right angles rather difficult. She has to land and start again facing in the required direction. The kitchen door opens outwards into the passage from the front hall. She has discovered that if she flies from the hall to the top of the open door she can then swoop into the kitchen without touching the ground.

With her increased flying prowess we feel that she is slightly less vulnerable to visiting cats; Moley we have no fears about—he still treats her with total disdain. But we still shut her in at night, just in case. It seems hard, since she would probably like to get up in the morning much earlier than we do.

She looks distinctly broody as dark begins to fall, and has to be put to bed smartly in the kitchen, usually on one of the chairs.

May 19th

Up until now, as it begins to get dark, I have carried her out and placed her on the short projecting platform in front of her little house. She walks straight in and settles down for the night, huddling herself up against the back wall, while I shut the wire door at the entrance. She has always waited for me to tell her where to go at bedtime.

This evening, however, as the sun was going down, I wanted to finish weeding the plant pots by the front door, so she decided to put herself to bed.

She jumped first onto the seat of the garden bench that stands on the porch about eight feet from her house, and some feet lower. Next she hopped onto the back of the bench, where she stood looking up at the entrance of her house, measuring by eye the distance that she had to fly. Then, after a great deal of shuffling from side to side, and a suggestion of spitting on the palms, she took off at too low an angle, hit the underside of the platform, and fell back fluttering to the back of the bench. She was now, however, facing the wrong way. She peered up and around her until she located the house again, and then very shakily, rather like a beginner on skis doing his first "kick-turn", she shuffled round to face it. She looked up at the platform, and you could almost hear her saying, "Right, misjudged that. Try again, but increase the angle."

I watched, fascinated, as she launched herself anew, and saw that like an inexperienced gun crew she had over-corrected, and this time landed safely but on the

17

pitched roof of her house. She registered surprise as she found herself facing a brick wall; she looked around, then turning she moved to the gable end and peering down she spotted the door below her. "Aha, there it is."

She flew back to the bench, turned round with much more confidence than before, and flew straight onto the platform. She looked at me over her shoulder as I burst into applause, and then passed through the little doorway. For some time I heard her squeaking and chuckling happily to herself before she settled down.

May 20th

Christian is home again, and introduced Victoria to the bird bath in the garden today. I photographed her as she waded around in the water. She seemed uncertain as to whether she liked it or not. She got fairly wet in the end, and I think Christian did too, but though I suppose she may be slightly cleaner she is still a very grubby-looking little pigeon, with a scraggy neck and very tatty feathers. She no longer has bare patches under her armpits, though, and all the unattractive yellow hairs have gone. She seems to be grey and black all over. If we had to pick up a pigeon in London, what a pity we didn't get one of the really pretty ones.

May 23rd

Victoria has taken to the bird bath and visits it on her own, though mainly for drinking purposes. I was watching her from the kitchen window standing in the water when a blackbird jumped onto the rim beside her. With a squeak of terror Victoria took off in disarray. I don't think she remembers even being so close to another bird before, and she finds it unnerving. Even sparrows alarm her, and she gives them a very wide berth.

May 27th

She has learned to identify the kitchen window from the outside, and will hop onto the sill and walk through to get her food, which is in a small bowl inside. Her favourite diet is now the hard dry peas of the kind consumed in vast quantities in Trafalgar Square, though she will also sample grains of wheat and small pieces of maize.

Today she was standing on the sill as I was waiting to shut the window, but wouldn't walk through.

"Hurry up, Victoria," I said, and to my surprise she turned and took off, out and high into the air in a great wide arc that took her far out above the garden and over the field beyond, and then back, fast and accurately onto the windowsill again. It was pure show-off —"Look what I can do!" I have never seen her fly so far or so high before, and she was enjoying the moment. Then she came in and had her meal.

Later in the day she was watching me as I worked among the young trees, basking in the sun and enjoying as I was the spring sunshine. I find the tree nursery much more appealing than my desk in this weather. Typing up minutes of charity meetings lacks attraction when the honeysuckle is coming out and the downs are glowing with colour. Victoria was on the ground near my feet when a pair of collared doves alighted in the branches of a small tree close to us. Victoria panicked and took off in flight, rather heavily and low above the ground, as she does when unable to time her take-off. The doves to my surprise pursued her, but higher in the air, and not with great enthusiasm. They gave up after a little, and flew off into the tall ashes down the hill, but I watched Victoria continue to take wild evasive action over the fields before she realised that she was no longer in danger. It is strange how nervous other birds make her.

May 29th

Victoria comes in the car with me sometimes. The first time I took her just for fun, and she seemed to enjoy it and find it quite unalarming. So now she takes it as natural that she should come, just as it comes naturally to take her. She sits on my knee or my shoulder, but if the dogs are not with me I put her in their space behind the back seat, where she pecks around and generally cleans up. The car is a Mini-clubman and used to transport everything from shopping to logs of wood and hay bales, so there is much scavenging to be done. However, the dogs, like all dogs, love to come as well, so then the rule is dogs in the back, where they sit obediently by the double doors, and birds in the front.

Jess and Cleo are rather alike to look at. They are both white with random black patches, and both half collie. Jess's other half is greyhound, and Cleo's is said to be Staffordshire bull terrier. To strangers, the only way of telling them apart is that Jess has a patch over her right eye and Cleo has one over her left. Most people think that they are related, but in fact all they have in common is that they both came, at different times, from the same dogs' home. There must be an amorous collie dog wandering around Sussex leaving his distinctive mark on the local puppies.

The two dogs make an eye-catching pair, and we are often asked what breed they are. A rather disdainful lady asked me this in Lewes some months ago, and I replied boldly that they were Hungarian Pointers. I saw the doubt in her eye as her mind riffled through the pages of the Kennel Club handbook, so I added, "Harlequin Hungarians, of course." Her face cleared, and she nodded. "How *very* interesting." The dogs moved as a perfect pair at my heels as we sailed off down the street. I suspect she was watching, but we didn't look back.

Today when I went shopping in Lewes I had the dogs in the back and Victoria in the front beside me; I left the car parked for about half an hour, and when I returned found them all three together in the narrow space at the back. Jess and Cleo, who normally lie down while they wait for me, were sitting upright, rather close together, by the rear doors. Victoria was lying down, very relaxed, just behind the seat. I was horrified by the thoughtless risk I had taken—Jess, after all, chases practically everything that moves, and is the terror of seagulls. However, at least we now know that the three of them are safe together, even at close quarters.

June 3rd

Tim points out that Victoria's squeak has gone. It has not been replaced by much sound, but one might say that there is an incipient "coo" there. She hums a bit, too, particularly when she is feeling relaxed, perhaps sitting on one of the kitchen chairs while I am cooking.

Deciding that she must become more independent, we are now leaving the door of her house open at night, so that she lets herself out in the morning rather earlier than we are prepared to do. Her developing ability in flight must make her less vulnerable to danger, and probably also means that she will leave us soon.

She turns up at the kitchen window around breakfast-time. As she usually then manages to stay indoors for a large portion of the day, her independence is not coming to much. She really likes being with people, whether they are outdoors or indoors.

June 5th

We are having the outside of the windows painted all round the house this month. Victoria finds this very entertaining, and joins the painters as soon as they arrive each morning, sitting on the roof of their van as they have their preliminary cup of tea. She keeps a close eye on them during the day, usually from the ground at the bottom of their ladders, while sifting through the scrapings of wood and paint as they fall. At times she flies up to the roof, and watches them from above.

This week we started putting her out of doors after her evening meal, which she usually has at about six o'clock, at the same time as Jess, Cleo and Moley. On the first evening she hung about rather pathetically on the windowsill, jumping up and down and tapping at the glass. Soon, however, she got the message, and as dusk fell she made her way round to the front and into her house.

In the morning, as soon as anyone comes into the kitchen, she lands on the windowsill and leaps around, flapping her wings at the glass, and tapping furiously with her beak. I found Moley sitting on the wide sill inside the window one morning, watching this display with a disdainful expression, while Victoria appeared not to understand why he didn't open up. When I did, she walked in and started eating her peas within inches of Moley's nose. He watched with disgust, then jumped down and walked away. Either he is not a proper cat or she is not a proper pigeon.

While we breakfast, Victoria walks about the table, pecking at the pattern on the cloth, and pruning the plant that sits in the middle. Its lower leaves have little chunks torn out of them all round.

June 8th

Imagine a connoisseur of precious stones, his magnifying lens screwed firmly into his eye, bending closely over a gem and peering into its depths for imperfections. This is Victoria examining any unusual object that she has not met before. Today she was fascinated by a tiny leech undulating its way across the roof of my Mini. She spotted it from the far side, and tacked across towards it, viewing it first with one eye, then with the other. Finally she bent over it, her head turned sideways so that she applied just her right eye, very closely for about a quarter of a minute. Then she straightened up abruptly and walked away. I had thought that she would eat it, but she never looked as if she intended to.

She loves car roofs—perhaps she likes the warmth left by the sun. She believes in inspecting the roofs of visiting vehicles, and then conferring her particular seal of approval, which is not necessarily popular. My own is covered with little mounds.

June 10th

Victoria came on an expedition with us today to see the gardens at Sheffield Park, which are ablaze at this time of year with rhododendrons and azaleas, a visual cacophony slightly mitigated by the spreading and softening of the colours in the water of the lakes. Victoria sat on my shoulder, and as we passed through the turnstile Tim heard another visitor say to a friend—"I expect it's a sort of National Trust advertisement—they're selling birdseed in the shop."

As we explored the woodland paths I occasionally put Victoria down to walk, but she made no effort to keep up, so in the end she spent most of the afternoon on my shoulder. She attracted some attention, of the "how sweet" kind. A small boy approached me at one point and said nervously, "You know, you've got a bird on your shoulder." It was irresistible to pretend that I hadn't noticed.

June 13th

We came home late one night, and we were surprised to find Victoria was not in her house. We assumed that she had got indoors, but could not find her roosting anywhere. We were not really worried, since she has slept indoors before, and you only discover where by the mess below her perch in the morning. However, next morning she was at the kitchen window as usual. This has happened three nights in a row, and the inside of her house now needs no cleaning, so she must have found somewhere else where she prefers to sleep. Is this the first definite sign that she is getting old enough to leave us? We will be rather sorry, as we enjoy having her around.

Even Alex, our elder son, who works in London and is only infrequently home at weekends, finds her interesting. Alex is not the most animal-conscious member of the family: years ago he asked our vet to "geld" his male guinea-pig when I objected to looking after its constantly reproduced progeny. In the event the vet complied, but we still decided to find another home for the guinea-pigs. But now Alex, older and wiser, shares my fascination and my surprise that a pigeon can be such fun.

June 14th

Victoria has met real danger for the first time. I met Jackie, who lives in the cottage up the hill from our house, walking through our garden, followed by her dogs and her cat. We were standing talking when suddenly the cat crouched and sprang, and we watched transfixed as it ran after Victoria, she flying low above the grass, her attempts to gain height frustrated by the cat's leaps at her back. Jackie and I both shouted, and I threw half an apple that I had been eating, which miraculously hit the cat and took its attention just long enough to allow poor Victoria to rise into the air. It was a near thing, but I hope it will serve to make her more wary of animals she doesn't know. The incident hasn't, however, altered her relationship with Moley.

June 16th

The painters, who only turn up when the weather is fine, and are therefore making very slow progress, complain that Victoria sits on their shoulders and chews their ears while they're painting. "That bird," they are calling her, which is a bad sign. I shall have to try to keep her with me during the day.

She can be quite aggressive at times, so I have a certain sympathy with her victims. She will sit quietly on your shoulder until you almost forget that she is there, and then suddenly she has grabbed your ear lobe and is trying to pull it off, shaking and tugging, and it is very painful. Or else she indulges in sudden violent jabs, most uncomfortable when they are actually in your earhole.

She has also taken a peculiar dislike to toes, bare ones, which she attacks with great ferocity and a sort of rumbling growl. She even attacks them when they are shod, which is less painful and quite funny, as if she is saying, "I know you are in there, even if I can't see you." But when one is lying on the lawn with bare feet it is better to cover them, in case of an unexpected attack.

June 17th

We have discovered where Victoria sleeps at night.
She has proved that she retains the soul of a true London pigeon: she has chosen for her permanent roost
the very noisiest place that could be found in this
peaceful country spot. She crouches at night on a high
stone ledge under the verandah on the garden side of
the house, as close as she can get to the outside telephone bell. This rings at such a pitch that it can summon me from down among the trees, hundreds of
yards away, when I am working outside. It must have a
positively explosive effect when it goes off six inches
from her ear, and yet she has chosen to sleep beside it!
Her behaviour is becoming curiouser and curiouser.

June 19th

At the week-end Christian and Daniel decided to teach Victoria to become a "homing" pigeon, and for some reason decided that she needed to do some high flying first. They took her out onto the roof and threw her out into space. The idea, they told me, was that she would circle round above them and then return. But instead it was like trying to throw a ball on an elastic string; however they threw her, she would shoot off about eight feet and shoot back just as fast. They gave up—you can't make anything return, they said, that won't go away.

The painters have reached the stage when they need to leave the windows partially open for the paint to dry, so that we shall not be sealed in. This gives Victoria ready and uncontrolled access to any room in the house, which is becoming rather trying. She flies around and settles upon things that should not be settled upon, like bits of china on mantelpieces. We have lost one or two things we liked, and one or two we didn't. On the whole I would rather know when and where she comes in. It is rather like having a very young child in the house who has no discrimination in what it touches or throws around. As with a very young child, you can't really scold a bird—you just have to take preventative measures. So the shelves and prominent places around the house are rather denuded of their nicer ornaments.

I found her in the kitchen after breakfast this morning standing knee-deep in an open box of Flora marga-

rine. She started guiltily and climbed out, walking along the work-surface and leaving a trail of sticky footprints. These presumably are also on the ledge above the door, where she went next, but I haven't looked to see. Apart from this kind of thing she is really very clean, and though you might expect to find a mass of unattractive bird messes about the house, all you ever find are small desiccated blobs, which are easily flicked away.

As I was sitting writing letters at the kitchen table later she walked about in front of me, eyeing my pen all the time. When I laid it down for a moment to look through some papers, she pounced furiously upon it, attacking it with her beak so that it bounced about, while she growled menacingly. I have seen her attack the telephone cord in the same way, and even bits of string—does she think that they are snakes, and dangerous, or worms, and edible?

June 22nd

Victoria loves the radio. I have Radio Four on a great deal, particularly when I am working in the kitchen. When there is only talk she gets on top of the set and walks about its short length, chuckling and mumbling. But when there is music on she listens in silence, standing in front of the speaker in rapt attention.

June 23rd

I examined Victoria closely today. She is definitely getting more mature and her feathers cover her more thoroughly, though not entirely smoothly yet. She is still a bit scruffy but she is certainly no longer a fledgling. On her neck there is beginning to appear a slight green sheen, which is a relief from the rather plain black and grey of the rest of her body. The paler grey markings on her wings are not unattractive. She is certainly getting the right food—you can hardly feel her breastbone now, and she is a positively plump little pigeon.

Despite her ability to fly as well now, I guess, as any adult bird, she stays around the house all the time, and only leaves it to follow someone walking away from it. If you plan to go in the car, she is always sitting on its roof before you get to it, in the hope of being taken for a ride. You can chase her off, but she returns as soon as you get inside. So then you have to do a racing start, or if that fails, brake hard, in order to dislodge her. This is necessary for any expedition when she cannot reasonably come along.

I was touched today to find her apparently waiting for me when I returned from London, sitting on a rose trellis halfway down the drive. I stopped to greet her, and she flew onto the roof. I drove on very slowly to the house to the sound of her feet pattering above me.

June 24th

A group of disabled people, mainly in wheel-chairs, came to visit us, and spent most of a lovely sunny afternoon in the garden. Victoria gave a lot of pleasure in the early stages, perching on the chairs and accepting little bits of bread, which she will not always do. But later she suddenly decided that she had had enough, and retired to the top of one of the garden sunshades, refusing to come down again. This was quite unlike her normal behaviour, and I wondered what had offended her. Perhaps someone had handled her in a way she didn't like.

It was quite strange that these people, who came from a home in inner London, where pigeons are the commonest birds about, should find one pigeon of such interest, and should show so much disappointment when she would no longer play with them. I think perhaps what makes Victoria special is that her behaviour seems in no way governed by a desire for food, but to stem from an interest in people, who she apparently finds a source of unending fascination.

June 30th

Victoria is beginning to lose her fear of other birds. I saw her taking her morning dip today, with several sparrows surrounding her in the bird bath, like a jacusi party, the spray created by their splashing water over their ruffled feathers. But her friends seem to be limited to sparrows and other small birds. She still reacts with alarm to anything larger, even pigeons, flying overhead, and doesn't relax until they are well away.

She enjoys other visitors, however, and has at last made good friends with the painters, who now call her by her name and try to share their sandwiches with her. They are finishing this week, and I think she will miss the activity outside the house. We will not.

She joins wholeheartedly in anything that goes on in the garden, and enlivened a meal we had with friends outside at the week-end. She made herself a nest in the crown of a straw hat left on a chair. When this was needed for wearing, she moved to a baby's pram and settled down on its hood, after peering down and inspecting closely the sleeping inmate, a smaller human than any she had previously encountered.

After lunch she followed us around the garden as she always does, sometimes walking alongside us, or running to catch up, sometimes sitting on a head or a shoulder, and moving from one person to another. People who don't know her often react with alarm when she first flies down to settle on their head, and then walk with stiff necks and glazed eyes as if fearful that she might fall off. Or else they bend their heads further and further forward, until she finds herself standing on the back of their necks. But they soon learn that if they simply behave as if she were not there life is simpler for everyone.

Just as she seems to enjoy being with us, I find her very good company when I am weeding in the garden or working in the tree nursery. Jess and Cleo are always with me too, of course, but they are constantly ranging around, hunting the rabbits that cause so much havoc among the trees and garden plants. Jess is very fast—a result of her semi-greyhound lineage. On holiday with us in Scotland she has on occasion run down a hare with ease, but is only interested in the capture, and not in the consumption, of her quarry. She is a dog of great elegance and dignity, and much is beneath her. If a box containing deliciously odorous sausages or chops is placed beside her in the car, she turns her head away with a "get thee behind me" expression, and indeed can safely be left alone with it. Jess is a bit of a goody-goody, but is still one of the most likeable dogs I have ever known.

While the dogs are hunting Victoria stays near me, perching on my behind when I bend down, which must look quite funny, or on the handle of my basket, which then falls over. She grabs bits of string and runs away with them, and when I am weeding she comes very close to my working fingers, nibbling at them as if she were trying to help them or find out what they are up to. Sometimes she darts at a weed I have thrown aside, and shakes it furiously.

I find myself talking to her as I work, which I think she likes, as sound always attracts her. When the dogs come bouncing back from a foray, she hops out of their way if they are being too boisterous, but is quite unafraid. Cleo, the more puppyish of the two, occasionally takes a bound at her, inviting her to play, but Victoria does not respond. She prefers to play with humans.

This is disappointing for Cleo. Being, at three years old, two years younger than Jess, her need for horse-play is greater than that of her more sedate friend. Victoria might have filled the gap.

Cleo and Polly, our youngest daughter, belong to each other. Polly is at boarding school, pursuing O levels, so during term time Cleo's devotion, which needs constant outlet, is transferred to Tim and me. She is a dog of extraordinary clumsiness and great charm. When emotionally overwrought, as when Polly comes home for a weekend, Cleo smiles, shutting her eyes and wrinkling her lips to bare all her teeth in an agony of ecstasy. She will also do this when scolded for some misdeed—for instance, unlike Jess, Cleo cannot be left safely in the vicinity for anything edible. Sometimes she will anticipate a scolding, and we only learn of the misdemeanour when Cleo walks into the room grinning.

July 8th

There is a change in Victoria that we did not expect. She is beginning to dislike being touched by hands. You can no longer pick her up easily; she evades outstretched fingers, although you can touch her with any other part of your anatomy without her minding. It is rather sad, but also rather inconvenient, because now if you want to move her out of a room you have to corner her, which is not always easy, as she knows exactly at what height she is out of reach.

But this dislike of hands apart she seems still to take pleasure in our company, and once caught, usually cornered on a windowsill, she shows no fear while being held, and if placed on a shoulder will stay there.

July 9th

Victoria, like all other pigeons I suppose, has most amazing eyesight. Or else she keeps a very close eye indeed on the garden side of the house in the early morning. The slightest movement, the least twitch of a curtain, brings her instantly onto the windowsill, flapping, jumping, tapping, demanding to be let into any bedroom whose occupant is showing signs of life.

If we decide to sleep late, say on a Sunday morning, she sometimes decides not to wait, and from about nine o'clock onwards on a sunny day we are aware of a little shadow bobbing about on the windowsill, and a gentle, intermittent tapping of her beak. But she doesn't start beating her wings against the glass until she actually hears us talking.

Christian always sleeps with her curtains and her window wide open, so when she is at home she tends to be woken rather earlier than the rest of us. She has complained of having her toes attacked when they stick out from under her duvet.

July 15th

I am beginning to wonder whether we should take out third party insurance on Victoria. I was taking an elderly female tree customer round the arboretum when this pigeon appeared out of nowhere and first buzzed her, then settled on her hair. The woman panicked, and screamed, waving her arms and hitting out wildly. Victoria, amazed, rapidly got out of range. I apologised and explained, but it did occur to me that we might have had a heart attack on our hands, which would have been embarrassing as well as bad for sales.

I can't help feeling that Victoria, if she is still with us then, is not going to enjoy the winter as much as the summer, when there is so much outdoor activity to share in. She helped me pick broad beans this morning, scavenging among the plants as I worked. I sat on a stone step in the sun, shelling them into a large Pyrex bowl. She perched on the edge of it, very wobbly, and leaned in to try and grab a bean. They were just too large for her to get hold of, and she couldn't quite spear them with her beak. Inevitably she slipped and fell in, and her legs sank into a pile of beans as if into a quicksand; she couldn't get enough purchase to climb out again, and looked silly and had to be rescued. She did all this again and again until, as I really wasn't making much progress as I was laughing so much, I gave her a handful of beans on the ground to play with. She didn't find this nearly so much fun, but she took the hint and wandered off to prune the long-suffering thyme on the flagstones.

July 17th

We think some bird may have attacked Victoria. She is looking very scraggy around the neck, as if something had grabbed her there and ended up with a mouthful of feathers. Perhaps she is only moulting—what time of year do birds moult?—but the moth-eaten look is rather too localised, I think, for that. I am reminded again of how little I know about pigeons. I should get a book, but probably shall not. I think advance knowledge would make her progress less fun to observe.

July 22nd

Malcolm and Ann, two old friends from London, spent the weekend here, and Victoria played a full part in all our activities as usual. The visitors found her very entertaining, and were intrigued by her constant attendance both in and out of doors. They got used to walking around with her sitting on their heads, and Malcolm posed for a Nelson-on-his-column photograph with her in the garden. She tasted his gin and tonic, and seemed to find it pleasing. I think we forget until strangers meet her that she is "quite an unusual pet," as someone described her. I rather hate the expression "pet," as I think of her more as an individual who has chosen to live with us.

Alex and Daniel were both home this weekend, and she joined them for a game of tennis, making quite a nuisance of herself. She insisted on perching on the middle of the net, unperturbed as they played over her, but rather putting them off their game. Later she moved off the court and onto the branch of a tree nearby. This must have been private territory, since she was mobbed by eight or ten sparrows. She rose high into the air with the smaller birds in pursuit, and then went spinning off into a clump of tall trees as she tried to evade them.

July 29th

Victoria is reported to have much upset Mrs. Taylor. She often flies down the hill to visit her house in the early morning. Evidently she entered one of her bedrooms by the window and left a trail of havoc before she was found. Mrs. Taylor is quite cross, I am told. I shall have to go and apologise.

July 30th

I took Victoria with me on a formal visit of apology. She was in one of her best moods, and both Mr. and Mrs. Taylor fell for her undeniable charm. All is forgiven, and Mrs. Taylor's windows are in future to be opened wide at night only! We are all adapting our lifestyles to accomodate this pigeon.

We have to warn our guests not to open their windows more than two inches if they do not wish to be assaulted in their beds in the early morning. So far they have taken it very well. In hot weather, when Tim and I have not been able to sleep with curtains drawn, our only hope in the morning is to hide completely under the duvet, since fingers and toes and ears are liable to attack. Once hidden, we can feel her pattering about on the duvet, looking for exposed flesh.

August 3rd

I was working at my desk until after Victoria's bedtime last night. I never allow her to be in the room when I am typing, since the sound of my electric typewriter is like a siren call to her, and her passage across the keys sends the machine into a frenzy of hyperactivity. This makes heavy demands on the corrector tape.

Thus I had forgotten the time, and found her sound asleep on a chair in the kitchen. She opened her eyes sleepily as I approached, but instead of evading my hands as she usually does now, she stepped onto my outstretched palm and allowed me to carry her outside. I put her onto her perch by the outside telephone bell. It started its extra-loud ringing as I did this, which startled me. But Victoria simply closed her eyes and fluffed her feathers out as she settled down again for the night.

August 8th

I have said before how much Victoria enjoys sitting on the roofs of cars. She has become quite adept at hanging on for a considerable time while they are in motion, and clearly enjoys a ride at least up to 15 mph. A visitor leaving the house a few days ago was unaware as he shot away down the drive of a small figure on his luggage rack, clinging to the front bar with both hands like a child on a roller-coaster. It was a wonderful sight.

August 10th

I came back from Brighton today to find a hilarious scene being enacted in front of the house. Stephen Phillips, agent for the Mid-Sussex constituency, had driven over in his Mini to drop some papers for Tim. He has the misfortune to be as nervous of birds as I am of scuttling black spiders, and hitherto I have protected him from Victoria. However in my absence Victoria had landed at once on his car, and had been holding him prisoner inside for some time. She was pattering backwards and forwards across his roof, bending down to peer at him through the windows, presumably wondering why on earth he didn't get out. I stifled my laughter while I grabbed Victoria and shut her in my car. Poor Stephen emerged pale and twittering with explanation.

September 8th

We went to Scotland as usual for our summer holiday. We considered taking Victoria with us, but decided against it. Kay Knowles, who lives in the flat at the end of our house, always kindly comes in to feed pigeon, goldfish, cat and dogs when I am in London on odd nights. She offered to look after Moley and Victoria while we were away. Jess and Cleo always come with us.

When we returned, after nearly three and a half weeks, we somehow expected that Victoria would be different, wilder perhaps, surely not so dependent on us. Kay had continued to fill her small dish of peas on our kitchen window-sill, but she would for a considerable portion of her short life have been out of daily contact with her human family.

We arrived home late at night, and Tim and I were woken the following morning by the familiar tapping and pattering at our bedroom window. How on earth did she know that we were home? Had she spotted that the curtains were drawn for the first time in three weeks, and come to a conclusion? Is a pigeon capable of reasoning?

I opened the window, and she hopped in and shot straight to the top of the wardrobe. She had indeed changed. For a start she was enormous. The threadbare look that we knew had completely gone; new, cleaner feathers seemed to have developed all over her, their soft colours blending into each other, the overall effect smooth and padded, a full size larger and very, very handsome. She was like a girl, last seen in tatty school uniform, who suddenly appears beautifully dressed as a fully grown adult, and makes you wonder where on earth she has been hiding it all.

The next shock came when she opened her mouth, as she strutted proudly about above our heads. Her voice had broken! Gone was the puny cooing that we knew: instead came a deep, rich rumbling sound, positively musical Rs rolled with resounding relish. I swear she was aware of the effect she was having, as we stood openmouthed gazing up at her, and she was loving it.

We inevitably have to speculate whether Victoria is indeed a "she." This huge creature has a much more masculine appearance and voice than the one we left behind in early August. We must find out what her sex is, but so far no one has been able to tell us.

September 12th

Music still has an interesting effect on Victoria, and she always tries to be as close as possible to the source of it. I often have the record player on while I am working in the house in the mornings. As this is in the sitting room she finds it rather frustrating, since it is a room I try to ban her from. She will sit on the sofa, and doesn't get off it to do her droppings. So I shut her in the kitchen, where she walks backwards and forwards along the bottom of the door into the sitting room trying to find a way through in order to get closer to the music. When I go through the door she tries to dash through on my heels, just like a dog, and when I come back she is waiting, and tries to squeeze past my feet. I have to open the door very gingerly, as she is usually close behind it.

September 15th

The small flower bed just below the kitchen window is producing a handsome crop of pea plants, growing presumably from the dried peas that Victoria constantly drops there. Perhaps she may in time become self-supporting.

September 18th

Victoria hates wet weather. At the first drop of rain she is at the kitchen window, jumping up and down, flapping her wings and banging at the glass with her beak. She is very unsociable when wet, and grumbles noisily on top of the cupboard as she dries off. This week she has a lot to complain about.

September 20th

A policeman came this morning to take a statement from me about a traffic misdemeanour that I had perpetrated some weeks ago.

We sat at the kitchen table, while I tried to remember times, road-signs and my possible motivation on the day in question. Suddenly, like Batman coming to the rescue, Victoria swooped in through the open window and onto the officer's shoulder. There she did everything she could to distract him from his task: she pecked his ear, she craned round and tried to peck his teeth and she hopped onto his head to give his hair a thorough going through. I didn't remove her, as I felt I needed all the help I could get, and soon she moved down his arm and went for his tunic buttons.

I was quite impressed by the officer's calm acceptance of the situation but he definitely wasn't melting. Victoria jumped onto the table and walked all over the paper he was writing on, making little runs at his pen.

I was very touched by the show of loyalty in my defence, but fear that I shall get a fine all the same.

After he had gone, she spent some time attacking the pen that lies beside the kitchen telephone. She pecked it, shook it, held it down while she tussled with it, and eventually knocked it, vanquished, to the floor. She definitely doesn't like pens and pencils.

September 25th

She took an evening stroll round the garden and the arboretum last night with Tim and me, attempting to ride on my head. She likes to use hair as a beak wipe. I jumped sideways once or twice to dislodge her, and after a little she understood. She followed along, waddling beside us as we walked. We agreed that she adds to the quality of our life. Her enjoyment in being close to people we find very endearing. Since she is never offered food except at her established mealtimes, morning and evening, her motive in following us can only be pleasure in our company, and we still find this surprising.

I was picking mulberries yesterday, working from the underside of the tree which is like an umbrella of closely packed leaves, with the fruit hanging inside them. Every now and then Victoria's head would pop through the leaves from the outside to inspect what my hands were doing. She is still very bad at telling which branch or twig will support her weight and which will drop her in an ignominious downward flutter.

September 29th

Cleo, who is a puppy at heart, still tries to get Victoria to play with her. She bounces hopefully towards her, with raised paws, but Victoria evades her, hopping a few feet forward or sideways as Cleo advances. It is not that she is frightened, it is just that she is not interested in that kind of game. On the other hand, when the dogs are hunting, looking for rabbits in the wood or along the hedges, she now likes to go with them, and follows them quite closely, watching their activities from nearby fenceposts. I took a photograph of her yesterday conducting the sport in the rough ground below the main arboretum.

There was heavy rain last night and it was still pouring at nine o'clock this morning. I called Victoria as usual from the window. Normally she is waiting, but if not, when I yell "Victoria," she appears at once. If she happens at the time to be on the other side of the house, she comes sailing over it, out high over the garden and the first field, taking a wide swing, and then at tremendous speed and with great accuracy lands on the window ledge with a thump. She loves showing off.

But this morning she didn't respond to my call, so I put on a raincoat and went round to the verandah. She usually leaves her roost at daybreak, but on this filthy morning she had obviously just decided to stay in bed, and instead of being bedraggled and miserable she was quite dry. She was not ill, as I had feared, just fed up. I invited her into the kitchen through the side door, which she appreciated.

October 2nd

Victoria would really like to be in the kitchen all day long, especially if someone is working in there.

Her favorite place is on top of the cupboard, which we have now covered with newspaper. She is very noisy when she first lands there, strutting around importantly with all her feathers pushed out, making her look half as big again, apparently establishing her territorial right with wonderful melodious rollings of her Rs. After a while she settles down, hidden from sight by the little parapet round the top of the cupboard, and we are only aware of her presence by the way she hums happily to herself, very quietly, a sound of supreme content.

But we try not to let her stay indoors too much of the time, because house-training does seem to be an impossibility. However she always gets in when everything is tight shut, like Macavity. Then she is incapable of concealing her whereabouts, and boasts loudly— "Here I am—I made it!" and gives herself away. She would crow, I believe, if she could.

Tim tells of following her upstairs to try to expel her. When he got to the landing there was no sign of her. He searched the bedrooms, and was just giving up and going downstairs again when she couldn't resist a triumphant purr from the top of the cupboard, and was spotted.

It is not always easy getting her out of doors. If she is in the mood, the words "Out, out, out!" said firmly and accompanied by a flapping hand will usually induce her to move towards the indicated window or door. But at other times, when the devil is in her, as it always is when you are in a hurry, you have to employ a tennis racquet or, in extremis, a long-handled broom to block her passage as she flies as close to the ceiling as she can. I dread the day when she discovers that the top of the pelmet above the curtains of the window in the well of the staircase is totally out of our reach. If she started to roost there we could have a very messy problem.

One night recently I made the mistake of letting her stay in the kitchen until after dark. I noticed her roosting above the door, sound asleep and with her eyes tight shut. I went and opened the window, and turned, saying "Out, Victoria, you can't sleep there." But she was already on top of the hanging corner cupboard, the most inaccessible place in the room, as she well knows. She's no fool.

October 3rd

It is very pleasant to be greeted by Victoria on arriving
home by car. She spots it as it approaches the house
and swoops down onto its roof, sometimes landing before it comes to a stand-still, and you can hear toenails
pattering about above your head. If the radio is on,
and particularly if it is playing music, she will drop
down onto the wing mirror and peer into the car with
her head on one side. Sometimes she sits on top of an
open car door; there is a danger that she may lose
some toes one day this way.

October 4th

I have observed a strange phenomenon. When Victoria walks, her head, like a hen's, moves rapidly backwards and forwards in time with her feet. When you pick her up, and you do the walking as you carry her, her head still makes this movement.

October 7th

We have been obliged to instal a telephone answering machine, mainly because my tree customers complain that they can never get in touch with me. It sits on the work-top by the kitchen telephone and we hadn't realised what a lot of fun Victoria would get out of it. Normally when a customer, or anyone else, rings, and I am talking wisely to them, Victoria likes to fly over and settle on my head as I talk, making crooning noises which I try to cover up with coughs. Now, when she hears the voice of a customer leaving a message, she jumps onto the machine and spins round, pecking hard at the plastic lid as if trying to get at the person speaking inside, clucking with disapproval. It is lucky, perhaps, that the customers do not know who is taking their order, since not all of them find Victoria amusing. Last week a man came to buy a tree, driving a very smart sports car, which clearly appealed to her as a potential chariot. When we had done our business, he drove off down the drive unaware that Victoria was clinging to the front of his roof-rack looking like a latter-day Boadicea. I don't know how he discovered that she was there, but a minute later he came up again, much slower, and backwards. Victoria was still in place, but looking back rather disconcertedly over her shoulder, like someone who has pressed the wrong button by mistake. The car stopped outside the house, and the driver got out and flapped her off the roof with his hand. She stalked crossly off round the corner of the house, leaving him examining his gleaming roof for clawmarks. I hid.

81

October 12th

Victoria has taken to drinking out of the goldfish tank in the kitchen. When she first started this, wobbling very precariously on its narrow edge, and flapping her wings a little to help her keep her balance, the goldfish used to dart frantically to and fro at the bottom, presumably thinking that she was a predatory heron. But now, after two or three weeks, though they still drop to the bottom of the tank, they no longer panic. She ignores them.

She got into the car again yesterday as I was preparing to go to Lewes, and so came with me. She really seems to enjoy car journeys. She usually sits on the back of the front passenger seat, or on the driver's shoulder, watching the other traffic on the road, and turning to look at anything that catches her attention. Sometimes she moves to the rear seat, when Cleo, sitting behind it with Jess, cannot resist sniffing her. Victoria doesn't like that.

On this occasion I took her to visit Vic at the corn merchants, who appeared surprised to see that she had survived. Once again he insisted on charging only a nominal amount for a large bag of pigeon food—"as she's a foundling," he said. He is going to get her a leg-tag from a pigeon-racing friend.

October 13th

I started making some curtains today, and Victoria greatly enjoyed helping. The sewing machine puzzled her—she perched on top of it, and bent down to watch the material passing under the needle. When she got bored with that, she got down and chased my plastic-headed pins around the table, and then started pulling them out of the material I had pinned.

To distract her, since she was distracting me, I put some music on the record player. She perched on the transparent plastic lid, and watched the turntable spinning beneath her for a little before she settled down to listen. She has always found Handel invigorating, and a session of "Water Music" kept her paddling around and chuckling appreciatively. Mozart, by contrast, she enjoys much more quietly, and this time she lowered herself into her feathers on the back of the red sofa, and listened with her eyes half shut. She may, of course, just have been sleepy. I am developing a dangerous tendency to anthropomorphise her.

I have never thought of the dogs in relation to music, I suppose because they never listen to it. I had a collie once, though, who would lie under the piano and howl, but only when one played the Eton Boating Song, and only if it was played in the key of G.

October 16th

I had no intention of taking Victoria in the car with me today, since I was going to a meeting in Uckfield, and would be out for two or three hours. For this reason I drove rather fast down the drive, and left her behind. When I was about half a mile along the main road I suddenly found her flying along beside the car. I stopped, and of course she landed on the roof, so I took her in as I felt it might be dangerous for her to follow me all the way to Uckfield. I left her in the car, parked in the street, while I was busy, and when I returned I found it surrounded by children, tapping on the glass. Victoria was not responding.

October 17th

The wet weather brings Victoria into the house more than ever, though we try to persuade her to stay out as much as possible. We still feel that we should not allow her to become too domesticated, in case she ever has to fend for herself. But I suspect that it is already too late, and she is an institutionalised pigeon.

She has found a new favourite place, which is inside the plaster horse's head in the kitchen. This is a full size replica of one of the Horses of the Moon that adorned the Parthenon until Lord Elgin removed them. It is made of plaster, and we found it in a junk shop in Thaxted years ago. It is fairly broken, but makes a rather pleasant ornament, sitting on top of the kitchen cupboard. However, it took Victoria to discover its true potential. It is hollow. She climbed into it one day from behind, where there is a large hole, and soon found that any sound made inside it is both magnified and enhanced. Now she spends hours sitting in it, out of sight, practising her rippling broken chords and filling the kitchen with happy sound. She has discovered the joy that others get from singing in the bath.

But having her in the kitchen is seldom total pleasure. For instance, she has removed virtually all the buds from the Christmas cactus, which had promised a magnificent display of flowers this year. And that was wanton destruction, since she didn't even eat them.

October 22nd

Kay described a lovely sight that met her as she came out of her sitting room in the flat today—Moley, the cat, walking down the passage towards her, followed by Jess, followed by Cleo, followed by Victoria, all in single file. Victoria often walks about the house like the other animals—yesterday I nearly trod on her in a dark corner. She should learn that the floor is not a very safe place for one so small. Nor are tops of doors. Polly failed to notice her on the kitchen door a few days ago, and Victoria didn't move fast enough as she shut it. She had a badly cut toe as a result, but Savlon and sympathy did wonders, and she is once again equally pigeon toed on both feet. Pigeons' middle toes really do point inwards.

I was going to a meeting in Petersfield today, and so was relieved not to see Victoria as I set off. However she soon saw me, and caught me up before I got to the bottom of the hill. But for once she was too clever, and shot off right-handed ahead of me, swinging towards Lewes, which is the way I usually turn. I turned left, and drove as fast as I could round the next bend, which is shrouded by trees and so escaped her. I felt rather mean afterwards.

When I returned some hours later, there was a car parked in the entrance to our driveway, and a man was bending over his open boot. I stopped, and got out to ask if he needed any help. In his boot was the enormous stuffed head of a lion. I said, "What a very odd thing to have in the boot of your car!" and he replied, "I suppose it is, but it's quite odd to have a pigeon on the bonnet of yours," which of course by then I had. *Touché*, really. I never did discover what he was doing.

October 30th

As Tim left the house this morning, he inadvertently allowed Victoria to slip in through the front door. Instead of flying straight up the staircase, as she now usually does, she joined me in the kitchen as I finished my breakfast. After eating hers on the windowsill, she flew around and settled on each of the familiar high points of the room in turn; then she alighted on the breakfast table, sending with her accompanying wind all my letters, bills and empty envelopes fluttering to the floor. Many of my sins of omission have for some time been attributable to Victoria, since not only letters but scraps of paper with vital telephone messages are now frequently found, too late, under the table, behind the curtains, or floating, illegible, in the goldish tank.

As I sat reading, she placed herself between me and the newspaper with apparent intention, moving, as I moved the paper, to continue the obstruction of my gaze. When I raised the paper so that I could read over her head, she hopped onto my wrist and walked up to my shoulder. There she sat gently and investigatively nibbling my ear, a not unpleasant sensation. A sudden violent peck, however, stung me into reaction—I took her beak between my finger and thumb and shook it, saying, "No, you wretched bird." As soon as I let go, she shot off to the top of the cupboard and rumbled in apparent outrage. Within seconds she was back, though, walking up my arm, pecking my ear (with no gentle preliminaries this time), receiving the same reprimand and retreating again to complain to the plaster horse. She repeated all this four times, and then, tiring of the game, settled down in front of me on the toast rack to do a bit of preening.

She gives meticulous attention to her feathers, which are now in the full beauty of adult plumage, very glossy and of wonderful variety in colour and marking. The soft blue-grey on her head gives way to rich pink and purple on her neck, shot with blue and green, the colour changing from one combination to the other as she turns her head and moves in the sunlight. Below her neck, down her back, white markings are finely drawn round the edges of the short grey feathers, becoming broader and bolder on the longer, darker feathers of her wings. Below the rosy swell of her breast, the colour fades again into the same soft grey of her head, and the bright pink of her legs and feet makes a pretty contrast.

She preens with quick, precise movements, darting at imperfections deep in the thick layers, and twisting her head completely round to reach her back. Then she selects a wing feather near the roots; it rustles as with one rapid movement she draws her beak down to its very tip, and then lets it snap back into place. Once her wings are both in order, she bends her neck sharply down to probe among the soft feathers on her breast, rearranging them busily like a Victorian lady fussing over her lace ruffles. Her toilet completed, she stands on one pink foot and very delicately scratches an ear with the other. At least I assume there is an ear buried somewhere in there behind her eye—her hearing is certainly very good.

November 4th

Victoria's preference for being indoors doesn't change. We never let her in—on purpose, that is—before nine o'clock, so in the early morning she goes visiting our neighbours; when she sees our curtains begin to open, from about eight, she tours the bedroom windowsills, begging to be allowed in to attend our washing, dressing and other activities. If she gets in illicitly, she can actually manage to spend a lot of time around the rooms and passages without being spotted as long as she keeps to her feet, but as soon as she takes to her wings the squeaking sound of her flight gives her away. I think she knows this, because she walks a great deal. We try, as far as we can control the situation, to confine her indoor activities to the kitchen, which is not always to her liking, since she really prefers to be where the action is. We do find, however, that her droppings, which appear at the rate of one per fifteen minutes, do less harm in the kitchen than elsewhere, since the surfaces and floor are designed for easy cleaning. This may sound unhygienic, but she seldom goes onto the work surfaces where the food is prepared, preferring the cupboard tops, which are now lined with paper, or the floor. The main exception to this is when she is stalking about on the table as we eat. She seldom tries our food, except for the sugar. She loves a taste from the sugar bowl, but occasionally gets the salt by mistake. Lately, though, she seems to be developing a taste for this too.

November 6th

On the subject of house-training, we have known for a while that this is impossible, not greatly to our surprise. We get a slight warning, in that she always takes two short steps backwards before defecating. This is not enough to be of use when she is on the table cloth, but a help if she is on your shoulder, and the adept, by a swift step forward, can avoid the worst. Surprisingly, despite the amount of time she spends on people's heads, particularly in the garden or when they are talking on the telephone, no one has yet to rush for the shampoo. Can it be that she has some delicacy? Or is it that her liking for inspecting and foraging in people's hair for edibles has led her to regard a head as a kind of feeding bowl?

It strikes me that birds have a great advantage over other non-house-trainable creatures, from the point of view of their human hosts, in that they have only one type of excretion and that non-liquid. If left alone it dries quite quickly to a powder which can be removed from any porous surface by the flick of a finger, leaving no stain. Persuading visitors of this fact is not always easy, but they do learn. Birds' droppings are also completely odour-free, another bonus, which almost makes up for having to keep rolls of loo paper especially for Victoria hidden at strategic points around the house.

November 11th

I have bought a radio for Victoria; it cost three pounds
in a charity shop, and has a good walking area and an
aerial, which she particularly likes. We are keeping it
in the kitchen, which makes her more willing to stay in
there alone. She likes to get on top of it, padding
round in circles if there is talk on, but usually sitting
down if there is just music. The aerial is about three
feet tall, and can be leaned out at any angle. Today
someone left it at about 45°, and Victoria flew to it and
tried to settle near the end. It subsided slowly to the
horizontal, she going down with it, as in a lift.

November 13th

Mr. Spencer, who is blind, came to tune the piano today. Mrs. Spencer brought him over by car, and left him working while she went to do some shopping. When I came in to give him a cup of coffee in the middle of the morning, he said, "Do you know you've got a pigeon in the house?"

Victoria had assisted at the piano tuning for some time, but eventually got bored. Mr. Spencer turned out to be an ex-president of a Sussex pigeon breeders' association, so I went and caught her and brought her to him. After handling her he said, "Yes, she's a nice little hen bird," and told me that she was definitely at least part racing pigeon. He also said that she would leave, suddenly, one day, as soon as the urge to breed came over her. I felt a pang of regret as he made this unemotional statement. I think that I have begun to forget that despite her oddity Victoria is a normal pigeon and may have normal pigeon needs. Still, I felt slightly hurt that Mr. Spencer should assume that she would throw us over so lightly.

November 16th

Victoria has developed an alarming new habit of flying just above or alongside the car, and then suddenly, without any warning, alighting on the ground in front of it, so that you have to stamp on the brake to avoid hitting her. Yesterday, when I was going down the drive in a hurry, she did this. I stopped, and then drove slowly forward, hoping to drive her on ahead of me. To my horror, she vanished from sight, and didn't reappear. I stopped again and, opening the door and bending down, peered under the car, terrified that I might find a flattened bundle of feathers. Instead I found myself nose to nose with Victoria, who was inspecting the exhaust system with apparent interest. So I drove on over her, and saw her in my rear view mirror walking forlornly back up the hill.

November 19th

I walked down to Mrs. Taylor's house to deliver her newspaper which I had collected with ours in the village, and found Victoria assisting some builders who are working at the house next door to the Taylors. She had evidently been there for about an hour, accompanying each barrow load of cement as it went round the building, either on the shoulder or head of the man pushing it, and surveying the work between times from the top of a pile of bricks. She was sitting there as I walked past.

, She reacted at once to my voice—or is it perhaps my appearance that she recognises?—and decided to come home with me. Usually she rides if there is a ride available, but today, the weather being fine and sunny, she thought she would walk. Her legs being rather shorter than mine, she tended to get left behind. Each time she had dropped back ten yards or so, because she had frequently to inspect some object she saw at the side of the road, she would make short low flights to catch me up, and then walk close beside me again. The dogs lingered a while by the builders, and when they came thundering up the hill together after us, passing within inches of Victoria, she behaved as if she didn't notice them, and they ignored her too. And yet they chase any other bird they see on the ground.

When we got to the house, she tried as usual to follow me through the door, which I prevented. But by the time I had got to the kitchen she was clamouring at the window, threatening to break her wings against the pane.

As usual, I found it hard to refuse her, and let her in, which I subsequently regretted, as she disturbed my lunch by removing the last buds from the Christmas cactus. She took an apparently malicious pleasure in evading my flapping hand, hopping just out of reach, and then returning to the attack as soon as I wasn't looking. She regularly prunes all the houseplants, which, apart from giving them a slightly moth-eaten appearance, probably does them no harm.

Eventually I switched on her radio, and after one or two changes of programme (she doesn't like French programmes—too much talk between the music) she settled down to listen. Radio Three suits her very well, and keeps her happy for a long time. Haydn and Mozart I consider to be her favourite composers, since she likes to listen to their music more quietly and for longer than to any other. Alex, though, assures me that she prefers the beat of pop music to anything else. I suppose we each find what we want to find in Victoria.

November 22nd

Victoria's passion for following the car took on a new and alarming aspect today. On my way to Lewes, I thought I had shaken her off before we reached the main road, but as I drove round the first bend I saw her flying beside me, on a level with the driver's window. Usually she turns for home about half a mile from the house, but this time she persisted. I began to slow down, then suddenly noticed what Victoria had not, that another car was overtaking me at speed. Its windscreen caught her from behind, and she shot straight up in the air and dropped over the hedge on my side.

I pulled up about a hundred yards further on and watched to see if she re-emerged. Two cars passed me going the other way and I saw their red brake lights come on as they got to the place where Victoria had been hit. I turned the car and drove back, fearful of finding either a road accident or a squashed Victoria, but to my relief found neither. Can one be prosecuted for not keeping a bird under proper care and control?

I was on my way to catch a train, so I didn't know until I got home the following evening whether she was all right, which she was. It ruined my trip to London.

November 25th

As I was preparing to leave this afternoon to fetch Polly for a long weekend out from school, Victoria was strutting about on the bonnet of the Mini, and I could see that she was preparing to tease me all the way down to the main road. So I opened the car door and left the radio playing while I locked up the house. She was sitting on the back of the passenger seat when I came back, so she came on the journey with me. On the whole her occasional droppings fall on the rubber mat behind the seat, as she always likes to face the way we are going; and if she sits on my shoulder as we drive she doesn't seem to do any droppings. We have noticed that over the last few months she has very seldom done a dropping on a person. I wonder, assuming that she is showing a certain discrimination, whether it would be possible to house-train her after all. I think it would take a lot of time and devotion. "I am so sorry, I am too busy at the moment house-training my pigeon." She could single-handedly turn one into an eccentric. I must fight against this. Perhaps it is too late.

November 29th

Again today, as I was taking Polly back to school, Victoria waddled along ahead, in front of the car, making it impossible for us to proceed down the hill. As soon as I stopped the car and opened the door, she came round to my side, hopped in, onto my right ankle, walked up my leg, through the spokes of the steering wheel and up onto my shoulder, where she turned round and settled down with a satisfied trill, which said so clearly, "Right, off we go!", that Polly and I both collapsed in laughter. It seems that the only way to avoid running her over and to prevent her causing other cars to crash is to let her have her way and always come in the car with us. This is blackmail—blackmail by pigeon! I swear she knows what she is doing, and what is more she has won. What shall I do when I am going to London, as I have to do more and more frequently now? I can't take her with me—or, appalling thought, is that what she really wants—to get back to her birthplace, her eponymous station?

December 2nd

Mr. Spencer the piano tuner has kindly sent me three split pigeon rings, a smaller version of the sort we used to put on hens. While Victoria was eating her breakfast this morning I wrote our name and telephone number on one of them with an indelible pen; it remains legible on the tree labels for a full season, so I doubt if she will be able to lick it off. When I had finished, I laid it down and walked round the table to collect her from the windowsill. Meanwhile, she hopped onto the other end of the table and crossed over to inspect the yellow plastic rings. They are no larger than the seeds of maize that she had just been gobbling, and to my alarm I saw one disappear in her beak. I yelled and thumped the table—the ring shot out as she flew, startled, to the top of the cupboard.

She didn't like the ring much when I put it on, but after ascertaining that she couldn't get it off she decided to tolerate it.

December 5th

This morning, as usual, Victoria flapped and tapped at the kitchen window, and on entry flew around the room, settling on all her usual perches in turn, noisily proclaiming possession of her territory. At each stop she fluffed out her feathers, doubling her size, and strutted about rumbling musically before flying on. Then she flew to the windowsill and ruined the splendid effect she was making by landing in the middle of her water bowl. She stood in it for a bit, as if trying to make it look as if she had done it on purpose. Having gorged herself on her dull dry mixture of brown peas, maize and wheat, she came back to the breakfast table, and standing close beside my plate, her head cocked on one side, closely inspected my face, before going about her usual business around the room. Today seemed to be the day for cleaning out the toaster, after admiring her reflection in its side.

December 7th

I put Victoria out of the window about mid-day today, and she had clearly forgotten during the morning what a windy day it was. As she flew from the sill a gust took her by surprise and she was blown ignominiously backward towards the berberis hedge. It has been mild so far, but she will learn some hard lessons this winter. I wonder sometimes whether we cosset her too much. She still sleeps outside on the ledge by the outdoor telephone bell, though I can't think how she can stand its shattering din so close to her ear, since it is twice as loud as a normal bell; but she does, as I have said so often, spend a lot of time indoors, particularly if it is wet, as she hates the rain. She will put herself to bed early on days when it is really wet. I am sure she should stay out more, to harden her up and make her more able to withstand the winter.

In fact, in these shorter days, she has to be out more, since she has to be in her roosting place before dark. If not, she seems incapable of finding her own way there; as darkness falls, sleep overtakes her wherever she happens to be. One day we were in Brighton together till after dark, and when we got home she was clearly all prepared to bed down on the back seat of the car for the night. I lifted her out, and since she never likes to be in your hand for longer than she need, I expected her to get onto my shoulder, or else to fly round the corner of the house by herself. But instead, and very unusually, she perched on my hand

like a hawk, and I walked round to her roosting place
with her. I had to shake her off to get her to perch on
the ledge—she might otherwise have come up to bed
with me.

December 9th

Victoria's interest in the making of the Christmas pudding made that somewhat over-rated pastime much more fun than usual. She was sitting on top of the corner cupboard in the kitchen, having a hum behind a large pottery chicken that is one of her favourite companions. She looked over its back and, seeing me collecting all the ingredients, bowls and spoons recommended by the Marks and Spencer cookery book, decided that this looked like her sort of fun. She swooped down from above, and landed on top of the bag of raisins, which skidded across the formica and collided with the large mixing bowl, saving her the indignity of being precipitated to the floor.

She watched closely while I poured, stirred and mixed, sometimes from my shoulder, sometimes from the counter as she strolled between bags of sugar, flour and dried fruit, and sometimes from the edge of the bowl itself. She tasted everything, but ate little. She drank some of the milk, and tried the brandy, which I had in a wine glass. This surprised her, and she retired behind the pottery chicken again, for a few minutes emitting a series of noises that I can only suppose were sneezes. Occasionally I could see her raising her head and shaking it hard.

She returned soon, and preened herself as I rolled out pastry for the mince pies, sitting very close to my busy hands. Occasionally she would break off and gently worry at my fingers with her beak—it is not pecking, but more like affectionate little cleaning mo-

tions concentrating on the base of my fingers and in between them. She has done this before, and it is definitely not related to food. I have wondered whether she is trying to help me with my preeing.

December 11th

I have discovered that Victoria's love of sound is not
indiscriminate. I was grating some very old cheese,
that had been in the fridge for a long time and was
distinctly hard at the edges, in order to make some
cheese straws. She was sitting on top of the plaster
horse when I started, and instantly became very agi-
tated. She flew from place to place round the room—
rarely settling for more than a few seconds, often
swooping close past my head, and in every way indi-
cating that she couldn't stand the noise and she wished
I would stop it. When I paused, she paused, and when
I started again she recommenced her frenzied circuit.
As soon as I finished my cheese grating she relaxed,
and got into her favoured place inside the plaster
horse's head, where she crooned consolingly to herself.
It is quite reasonable to suppose that a bird as musically conscious as she, who appears to differentiate if
not between composers at least between musical
styles, should have sensitive hearing, and cheese grating must be to her like finger-nails on a blackboard to
others.

December 13th

Some neighbours who live about a quarter of a mile away telephoned today to say that they had a pigeon in their house with our telephone number on it. I think they were a little disappointed to find that she lived so close. I am relieved, though, to know that people react to the ring on her leg. If anything ever happens to her we will now have much more chance of hearing of it.

I would miss her very much if she were no longer there. She is such a charming companion, unpredictable and funny, and it is very pleasant to be greeted on arriving home by her landing on the roof of the car as she joins you for the last few hundred yards. She seldom misses an arrival.

December 17th

Victoria doesn't get any less clumsy as she moves around the house, or really learn very much from her mistakes, which is why we are all constantly laughing at the things she does. For instance, when she lands on the formica surface of the kitchen furniture she skids into whatever is sitting on it, rather like a not very good skier showing off as he arrives outside a crowded restaurant, misjudging his final flourish and crashing into the deck-chairs. Victoria's mishaps cause the same hilarity among the onlookers. Today, planning perhaps to avoid this humiliation, she landed on a newspaper, which acted as a toboggan, and she and the newspaper shot off the formica and crashed together to the floor. She grumbled huffily to the plaster horse for several minutes.

December 20th

I am getting better at sneaking away in the car while Victoria is busy indoors; but she spotted me leaving today, and caught me up a mile down the road. Although she flies close to the car as it leaves the house, now she often goes above the taller trees that close in over the route, and rejoins you when the road is clearer. Then, of course, she swoops down, and I always feel I must stop for fear that she is hit by me or someone else, and she joins me in the car.

Coming back to where it is parked after shopping, you usually find a little group of children, and sometime adults too, bending down and peering at Victoria as she sits on the back of the driver's seat, studiously ignoring them. When you climb in, she hops onto your shoulder, and you can almost hear her saying, "I've had enough of this—let's go."

She never tries to get out of the car until we get home, though she will sometimes alight at Mrs. Taylor's house while I am delivering the newspaper.

December 21st

Victoria and I went to the village together today. She was on my shoulder as I drove, and stayed there as I went into Mrs. Cornwell's to collect the newspapers. I introduced her to Mrs. Cornwell, who looked politely bemused, while Victoria looked the other way. As we came out, an enormous lorry thundered by, and Victoria shot up in the air in apparent alarm; she disappeared high above the road, travelling in the direction of Lewes. I thought of following her, but decided to go home instead. As I pulled up in front of the house she landed on the bonnet. I think I can stop fussing.

December 24th

All the family is home. The gathering of holly and the decorating of the Christmas tree involved a lot of opening and shutting of the front door, and every time it was left open a small grey figure came waddling in to try to join the party. She was several times persuaded to turn round and waddle out again, but eventually we gave up. She pecked at the holly berries on the floor —there are very few this year, and she may have noticed among them cotoneaster berries masquerading as holly. She showed no great interest in the Christmas tree decorations; she has never identified much with trees, and this was just another one, and in the wrong place anyway.

Tim told us of a fright as he drove to Lewes today. Victoria had followed, and as they went along the main road overtook the car at head height and flew straight onto the bonnet of another car coming the other way, as the driver braked in alarm. There was no accident, but there easily might have been. We will have to be much more careful to take her with us or make sure she stays at home.

Christmas Day

Victoria received (her only Christmas present) a bell made of seeds designed more for budgies than for pigeons. It was hung at eating height from the lamp that hangs over the kitchen table; but, despite practical demonstrations by the boys of how it could be grabbed in the teeth and chewed, Victoria would do no more than look at it, her head cocked sideways, suspicious and unimpressed. She prefers our toast, though she will not eat crumbs, but likes to be given a whole slice, which she attacks with gusto standing on it the while to hold it down.

There was a move to take her to church with us, but this was foiled.

December 28th

Yesterday Victoria did not come when I called her from the window at breakfast time. I thought perhaps she was visiting the builders who have been working down the road lately, but I realised later in the morning that they have not been there since before Christmas.

By mid-morning it was clear that something had happened to her and I started telephoning neighbours. Mrs. Taylor said that Victoria had called on her as usual at about 8 a.m., but had not come in, and she hadn't seen her since.

After lunch we all went out to search, but I think we all felt that we were not going to find her. We had never had to look for her before. We opened the door of every place where she could possibly have got shut in, and some where she could not, with thoughts of the fate of the bride in *The Mistletoe Bride*.

There were people shooting in the wood on the downs above the house, but they didn't start until mid-afternoon, and she had disappeared much earlier.

Just before dusk I walked again through the strip of wood between the house and the road, and met separately two other members of the family who had slipped away to search on their own. We all mind. During the evening I think everyone must have gone quietly out to check her roosting place, without any real hope of finding her there.

December 29th

The fact that she has our telephone number on the ring on her leg makes me very conscious of a surge of hope every time the telephone rings. But I think they would have rung by now.

Today we searched along the main road, for half a mile in both directions, and in the hedges and fields alongside it. Perhaps she played "chicken" just once too often. It was hard to know whether we were hoping or not hoping to find a little pile of grey feathers. In any case, we found nothing.

January 3rd

I have found it hard to continue my diary.

We have all now reluctantly accepted that Victoria is dead. This loss overlays everything I do with a dull ache. I find myself quite unable to talk about her, or to join in discussions at mealtimes as to what might have happened on the morning of December 27th. I think I am fearful of revealing, even to myself, the fact that an ordinary London pigeon has left such a gap in heart and household. I really think if I take the lid off I might cry, and that would be silly.

I didn't notice as it was happening the change in her position with us. At the start when she came unexpectedly into our busy life, she was just another thing to cope with, to fit between meetings, tree work, rushing up and down from London, influxes of visitors and ordinary family problems. Then, as her development began to intrigue me, recording her life became a new interest, a quiet and enjoyable thing to do late in the evenings. I wasn't aware until now that she had gradually made herself an indispensable member of the family. She was, after all, only a pigeon.

I am shocked and embarrassed by the sense of desolation that I feel.

January 5th

Last night I dreamed that we were walking on the downs, all seven of us, as we occasionally do when the whole family is at home. Victoria was with us, sometimes riding on our shoulders, sometimes walking beside us, lagging behind and making short, low flights to catch us up. We came to a pond surrounded by trees. A strange dog ran at Victoria, and she took off and flew low over the pond, landing in the water a few feet from the further shore. For some seconds she floated on the surface like a seagull, but then she sank. I ran round the pond and dived in. I caught her in my hand, a foot or two below the surface.

We climbed out again—I was dry, but she was wet and bedraggled, looking very like the fledgling we found in Victoria station, and shivering. To warm her, I held her inside my coat in my cupped right hand, her head looking out over my wrist. I could feel her heart beating.

As I woke up, and even as I was taking in this cold grey morning, the dream seemed real in my sleepy mind. I found that I was still holding my cupped hand tight against my ribs. But there was nothing in it.

About the Author

Alice Renton's life has been too fully occupied until now to allow her to write. Her husband, Timothy Renton, is a Member of Parliament and Parliamentary Under-Secretary of State for the Foreign Commonwealth Office; they have two sons and three daughters; and they grow and sell trees. However, Mrs. Renton enjoyed keeping her Victoria diary so much that she has since embarked on a collection of stories, all of them concerned with life on an island off the coast of Scotland, which she knows very well. Another book, she reports, is waiting in the wings.